Thirty Days of Inspiration
VOLUME I

w/
Author
Angel Ferguson

ISBN-13: 978-0692720295 (Custom)
ISBN-10: 0692720294

Wisdom worth sharing………………………….

One day I discovered that
if I let go I would gain so much more!

I learned of my purpose,
so I let go of the thought
that I did not belong upon this earth.

I learned to accept me,
so I let go of the image that I was not good enough.

I understood that I was loved,
so I let go of the thought that I had no love to give.

I learned to listen,
so I let go of the thought that I had nothing to say!

I learned that if I would step out of my own way
that my possibilities became unlimited,

so I did just that,
I let go of what I thought of me
and accepted
what I was created to be……………………..

Stay encouraged family,
encouraging others along the way!

Life has taught me
that in order to accept the reality of me
that I must first face & overcome
the fears that I once hid behind.

The truth of the matter is this,
although I may know of my purpose in this life,
if I am in fear of moving forward,
my purpose will not come forth!

Fear is simply a set-up
to keep you from fulfilling your dreams & goals!

Let us learn to be
as we were destined to become
knowing that we are
more than conquers in Christ!

Keys of life worth sharing,

Self-doubt is our biggest struggle
not your fellow man...........................

Your survival is not based off of
the approval of others
but of the love, acceptance & belief
you have in yourself!

I believe in the potential of you,
now it's time to start believing in you too!

Life's lessons has taught me
that there is no difference
when being in a struggle
or when I am being tested,
when the common detonator is
MATURITY!

I am simply a product of my
mindset...

Maturity has taught me
that I can offer no excuses
for my lack of anything
if I have not applied the gifts given unto me!

In this life,
I have learned to hold my hand out
for an understanding
& that I am equipped
to go after the things
that are within me
that will guarantee my survival
rather than the expectation of others
to hand things unto me so freely!

I can become either my excuse
or my

solution………………..

I choose the latter.
What choice will you make?

Though we have moments of darkness
and those times that
seem to come up against us,
I believe that things will get better
if we keep our focus on
what is waiting for us in the long run!

Ask yourself, if you give up now,
whom did you fail,
whom did it affect
&
where was your faith!...................

For I have an understanding
that if it is easy,
it is not a test to my maturity
but an addition to my ego!

For if at one time
you imagined that your dreams
were all about you,
then I have come to inform you, they are not.

Our purpose upon this earth
was never to just keep
the lessons learned to ourselves
but too share & inspire them with others
both near & far.

The reality of life is
that we are trained to think & say
that our past does not define who we are today.

But the truth is this, it does!
It is the things of our past
that has shaped us into who we are
as well as who we desire to become in the future.

Never become ashamed
of the lessons life has taught you,
but become ashamed
if you did not apply
what was taught
so that you can make better decisions!

Stay encouraged, encouraging others along the way!

We keep hanging onto words
yet fail to have any expectations of any actions!

The cheapest thing one can do is talk,
put some movement behind you,
then you will gain the attention of a multitude!

When you can gain the understanding
of the true meaning of
After The Morning After,
you will stop rushing through the night!

For during the night
is where I become equipped
for the things that are ahead!

Each new morning
is another grand opportunity
for a powerful impact!

Good morning, Make it a great day everyone.

For so long
we've trusted the concept
that if I hold on I have control
but the reality is this,
learn to let go
to see if things
can stand up on
their own!

It's easy to dream
and even easier to talk.
The truth of the matter is
that's it is even easy
to take some course of action.
The power to remain effective
is to have endurance
& belief in the dream
that you have talked about.

The love of my dreams
& the focus of my goals
is what keeps me coming back for more!
When you realize your drive,
you will not allow
anything to stand in your way!

No morning is the same,
it's what you put in to each day
that matters.
Yesterday I was,
today I am
&
with Faith tomorrow I shall be!

Never allow the passion
for your dreams
to burn.............................

Keep the flames ignited
by pouring life into them daily.

Your dreams will only
live,
grow
and multiply
when they are fed
with a mass of positivity from you!

Learning
to rise
with new ambitions
&
great expectations!

Simply encouraging each of you,

the next time you look

at your circumstances

and begin to question how and why………

Here is the answer

that can only come from within in,

I am the results of my expectations"!

The truth about life
is that it will not lead you
where you're not willing to go!

We have a choice
to take the path
being presented
or too travel
the roads predestined
& desired……………………………

To say that life
has dealt us an unfair hand
is false because
it was you
that decided to play
the unbalanced game.

I love you family without measure & limits!

We came,

we saw,

we learned,

we laughed,

we cried,

we shared,

we grew,

we moved

on...

we repeated this process

because this is what you call life!

Learn to live it

without measure

or with no hidden agendas!

As the days are surely to change

from night into day,

I am sending out this question,

"What is your turning point"?

Shall I allow my dreams to live

or let them die?

Shall I continue to settle

for less because someone said

that's all I can have or am worth?

Are you your great potential

or are you the negative opinion?

Simply reminding you

that you are what you desire to be,

just put some positive actions behind it

to make it happen!

Sending these words your way!

Stay encouraged

as there is a purpose

for the storm that you're in.

It's a part of the process

of moving you to the next

level& phase of your life!

I am learning not to fight

the storms

but to understand

the strong gusty winds

& the hard down pour of the rain!

I'm learning

to take notice of the atmosphere

after all has ceased

& what was removed from my trees of life

& what has fallen to the ground

& what has remained!

Before you decide to give up

on your dreams,

thinking that you have failed,

ask yourself

if you actually really tried!

When you can finally understand why those that you depended on the most were no longer there!

It's because God wanted you to put

& keep your faith in Him

and not on the promises of

man..............................

We all must learn to walk alone

before we can walk in a group.

Often times we hear people talk
about following your dreams
but have failed

to tell us that in order to follow those
dreams we must have a vision.

So my question to you today is this,

do you have a vision for the dreams

that you have

that will lead you to your goals?

I truly believe and stand on these words "
Where there is no vision, the people perish"

as well as

" Write the vision and make it plain"

Simply put, you must have an outline of
what you want the end results to be.

You must also have a plan of action of how
to make it a reality!

Don't just jump in the sea, expecting to get
to the other side, take the time to charter a
boat with an experienced captain!

As I am bringing my morning under control,
these words fell on my mind.

Some may ask "what inspires you"?

Well it's the days of my past

that causes me to push for better!

It is those moments of being disappointed
that says,

yes I have control of the outcome!

Simply encouraging each of you that
there are times that

you must encourage yourself!

Learn to speak positive to yourself!

Encourage yourself to move forward
& stop settling for less!

Learn to stop crying because of hurt but because
you were able to take that hurt and turn it into a
positive move in your life!

Let's do more than shake that feeling of despair
but move far from it, learn to place yourself in a
positive atmosphere.

Take this day to observe those around you and
those you communicate with, if you can't hear
anything positive within the first few words
MOVE!

Count it all joy

when it comes to

every effort you make

towards your dreams!

Every small step

towards your destiny

is another piece of the puzzle

that will one day

display the big picture of your purpose!

It's true that better days are ahead,

but you must go after them!

I am in the mist of tracing my steps

not to relive the pain & disappointments

`but to make sure that

I don't repeat the things

done on my part

that caused the

pain & disappointments experienced!

Once we can grasp the understanding

that our journey

is not about correcting others

but only ourselves,

we will all become a much better people!

If you feed a dream,

it will grow!

If you invest in your purpose

it will live!

And if you inspire others

you're fulfilling His Mission!

Enjoy your Friday family &

Invest in it what you will!

When you realize

the hole you've been digging

for someone else

is actually your own,

you'll throw the shovel away!
There is no benefit

in causing others any harm.....................

I am sitting here thinking
of the things done yesterday
and this question came to my mind,
where will my decisions of yesterday lead me?
Better yet,
who will become affected
by my decisions of yesterday,
and who will benefit
of my path being taken today?
Never become fooled
or misguided that we are not responsible
for our yesterdays! Just don't allow it to become
your chains of bondage….
My soul is heavy as I think of the warnings
we receive yet continue to ignore them.

There is caution in the winds of our lives, I am learning to slow down and listen. Talking to my mother the other day and these words are still lingering " there is a reason that the red flags appear! They are there to remove the blinders before the unsteady clouds blind us permanently". Maturity calls for caution, just as the errors of my yesterday has caused me to think before I move. Simply encouraging you this day, not to ignore those things that we often take as small clashes of nature…..as the clash is a caution of being unbalanced down the road.

There is something special

when all things come together as one!

One thing is for sure,

when you have gained an understanding

of your rhythm

& the words began to make sense,

I say you have become one

with your journey!

Live Laugh & Inspire someone today!

If you can survive those bumps &
bruises of life,

know that you can survive

the curves as well!

Keep pushing forward.

We pray that you have enjoyed Volume I
of Thirty Days of Inspiration
w/ Author Angel Ferguson

Please allow us to leave you with the words, until
the next volume………………..

Life is an opportunity given.
Yet the question remains,
what are you going to give life?
Keep your anguish
and complaints as there is enough of that!
Please don't share
your negativity
as we've seen enough of that as well!
Take from life what you will,
just remember life will only give you
what you have given it!
I choose to give the potential
God gave ME
this day & every day that I am granted to see life.

www.ingramcontent.com/pod-product-compliance
Lightning Source LLC
Chambersburg PA
CBHW041809040426
42449CB00001B/24